ROTHERHAM LIBRARY & INFORMATION SERVICES

This book must be returned by the date specified at the time of issue as the Date Due for Return.

The loan may be extended (personally, by post or telephone) for a further period, if the book is not required by another reader, by quoting the above number.

LM1(C)

Heat

written by Maria Gordon
and
illustrated by Mike Gordon

Wayland

Simple Science

Series Editor: Catherine Baxter

Advice given by Audrey Randall - member of the Science
Working Group for the National Curriculum.

First published in 1995 by
Wayland (Publishers) Ltd
61 Western Road, Hove
East Sussex, BN3 1JD, England

British Library Cataloguing in Publication Data
Gordon, Maria
Heat. - (Simple Science Series)
I. Title II. Gordon, Mike III. Series
543

ISBN 0 7502 1293 4

Typeset by Macguru
Printed and bound in Italy by G Canale and C.S.p.A, Turin, Italy

Contents

Heat is a sort of energy.
It is called energy
because it makes
things happen.

Heat can make soft
things hard... and
hard things soft.

Heat is... the warmth of the sun... the feel of hot potatoes... and even of each other!

The sun heats the whole world. But some parts of the world are hotter than others.

The Earth is round. The parts around its middle are nearest the sun. They get more heat.

The sun sends out heat that people, plants and animals need to live. Heat comes from volcanoes, hot springs and lightning too.

 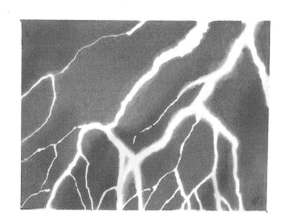

People have found many ways to make heat for themselves. How many ways can you see here? How is the heat being used?

Cave people rubbed sticks or stones together to make fires from wood.

The fire scared dangerous animals away, kept the people warm and cooked their food.

Later, people learnt how to burn oil and coal for cooking and heating.

The Romans even heated houses and swimming pools by sending hot air under floors.

You can make heat by friction. This means rubbing things together. Rub your hands together and feel the heat.

You can also make heat using pressure.

Press two ice cubes together. They warm up and melt where they touch. Stop pressing and they freeze again and stick together!

12

Switch on a lamp. Do not touch it, but *feel* around it. Electricity makes the bulb get hot inside.

Watch steam coming out of a compost heap. Heat is made when things rot!

When many things get very hot, they mix with air and make fire. This is called burning. Something that burns is called fuel. Wood, coal, oil, gas and petrol are all fuels.

Watch a grown-up burn a match. The match is made of wood. See how the wood turns soft and black. You can't use the match again!

Fuels can only be used once. We must be careful not to use them all up.

Heat is always moving. It flows from warmer things to cooler things.

Put three bowls on a table. Ask a grown-up to fill the left bowl with cold water and the right bowl with hot water. Fill the middle bowl with warm water.

HOT

WARM

COLD

Put your left hand in the cold water for about a minute.

Your hand feels cold because heat flows out of it into the cooler water.

At the same time, put your right hand in the hot water. The heat flows from the water to your hand. Your hand feels hot.

18

Now put both hands into the middle bowl.
The water feels warm to your left hand, but
cold to your right hand!

Heat is flowing from the water into your left
hand, but it is flowing out of
your right hand.

Heat flows through some things better than others. Touch an ice cube with a pencil. Your fingers do not feel much different. Heat does not flow well through wood.

Now touch the cube with a coin. Your fingers feel very cold. Metal lets heat flow through it very well.

PHEW!

Heat does not flow well through air. Air helps keep things warm.

Wool and fur trap air between their tiny hairs.

The tiny holes inside a styrofoam cup hold air.

Heat makes many things change. Leave some chocolate on a saucer in the sun. Watch the chocolate melt. Heat flows into it.

Put the chocolate in a fridge. The heat flows out of it and it gets hard again.

Ask a grown-up to help you make some cake mixture. Pour the mixture into a tin and put it in the oven.

The heat from the oven makes the mixture firmer.

The cooked cake mixture is not like the chocolate. It doesn't change back when it cools down.

Heat makes many things stretch. Look at a glass thermometer. The red or silver line stretches when it gets warm.

BODY HEAT
98·6°F

This is how a thermometer measures how hot things are. It measures temperature.

FREEZING
32°F

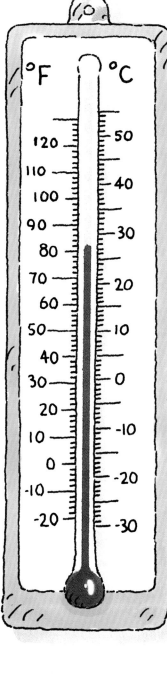

°F   °C

120 —   — 50
110 —
100 —   — 40
90 —   — 30
80 —
70 —   — 20
60 —
50 —   — 10
40 —
30 —   — 0
20 —
10 —   — -10
0 —
-10 —   — -20
-20 —   — -30

Cold things have a low temperature.

Hot things have a high temperature.

Ask a grown-up to help you measure the temperature of different things.

The food you eat makes heat inside you. You can die if you get too hot or too cold. If you didn't sweat you could bake. If you didn't wear clothes you could freeze.

Animals' bodies have different ways to keep cool or stay warm. Polar bears would freeze if they didn't have thick fur coats.

But if elephants had fur they would bake. Their enormous ears help them to lose heat.

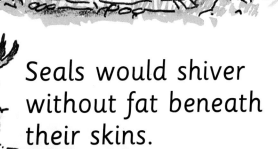

Seals would shiver without fat beneath their skins.

Burning too much fuel in the world makes the air thicker. This makes it hold too much heat.

The extra heat could hurt people, plants and animals. It could melt the North and South Poles, too. This would make the seas flood and cover the land where people live and plants grow.

One way that we can stop this happening is by using the sun's heat to make electricity. In sunny places, solar panels are used to make enough electricity to supply whole houses.

You can do your bit too by saving heat energy.

What ways can you see heat being saved here?

Notes for adults

The Simple Science series helps children to reach Key Stage 1 Attainment Targets 1-4 of Science in the National Curriculum. Below are some suggestions to help complement and extend the learning in this book.

4/5   Write poems about the pictures. Note the colours in the scenes. When and why do people feel hot and cold?

6/7   Read the legend of Icarus. Make a photo display of people and plants in different countries. How do the people dress? Use a globe. Investigate seasons.

8/9   Make a mini-greenhouse with a glass jar over grass on a lawn. Compare growth with uncovered grass. Visit forges, glassworks, potteries and greenhouses. Investigate use of infra-red in rescue operations.

10/11   Investigate natural fires and their consequences. What might cave people have learnt from them? Draw with charcoal, hold a barbecue, scrub with pumice stone.

12/13   Feel the heat from a bicycle pump in action. Look out for shooting stars burning because of friction with the atmosphere. Do a safety project on house fires.

14/15   Make a chart showing fuels used at home and school. Look at the consequences of fuel extraction, transportation and use – eg mining, oil slicks, smog.

16/17   Watch birds riding thermals. Feel the side of a fridge. Discuss cold as lack of heat.

18/19   How quickly do ice cubes melt at different distances from different sources of heat?

20/21	Compare ice cubes in sunshine under black cloths and white cloths. Use Thermos flasks. Spot insulation in use at home and school. Feel fur and feathers. Use oven gloves.
22/23	Use ice and wax too. Discuss the three states of matter. Make and bake clay models.
24/25	Research Gabriel Fahrenheit. Demonstrate cakes rising. Measure temperature indoors and outdoors and in baths and swimming pools.
26/27	Read Hans Christian Andersen's, 'The Little Match Girl'. Make a display of warm and cold-blooded animals. Discuss the differences.
28/29	Borrow a solar panel. Make a display of sun safety items eg creams, parasols, sunglasses. Paint pictures of polluted and clean futures – compare them. Investigate geothermal plants and heat from waste. Introduce simple conservation measures – even heat from rabbits in hutches has been used for greenhouses!

Other books to read

Fire by Gabrielle Woolfit (Wayland, 1992)

Global Warming by Laurence Pringle (Hodder & Stoughton, 1990)

Hot and Cold by K. Davies and W. Oldfield (Wayland, 1991)

Hot and Cold Places series (Wayland, 1994)

My Science Book of Hot and Cold (Dorling Kindersley, 1992)

Index